Stock Explore

Written by Nicolette DiMaggio   Illustrated by Ethan Roffler

Published by Stock Explore LLC
Copyright © #TXu2-142-555
ISBN: 978-1-7359706-1-5

Illustrations and layout by Stories Untold LLC

To my grandfather Richard Carravone (Poppy). Thank you for encouraging me to invest and driving me to elementary school. You are the smartest man I know.

One sunny afternoon, Elle asked Sam the Owl, "What is a stock?"
Sam the Owl replied, "A stock is a piece of ownership in a company."

"So, I own this company now?" asked Elle. "SWEET! I knew I would be a boss one day."

"No," said Sam. "You own a piece of the company, Elle."

"Well, what can I possibly do with that?" she asked. "You know I always appreciate your advice, Sam, but I can't eat a piece of a company, I can't see it and it is certainly not fashionable... I just don't understand how owning this stock benefits me at all."

"Elle, trust me," said Sam. "This is the most valuable lesson I've ever shared with you. Owning stock gives you the right to vote on company decisions, along with those who own the remaining pieces of a company."

"Okay, so I have voting power," said Elle. "What else?"

6

"As the company grows and gains in value, your stock will grow in value with it," replied Sam. "This will make you wealthier and will also play a role in the company's growth and success."

"But not all companies are successful," said Elle. "What if the company shrinks or goes out of business?"

"Good question, Elle!" exclaimed Sam. "If that happens, your share will decrease in value or become worthless."

"Oh, that would be terrible!" said Elle. "How do I know if this company's value will increase or decrease?"

"Ah-ha! Another good question, Elle," said Sam. "No one has a crystal ball that can predict the future success or failure of a company. But a good place to start is by learning financial statement analysis!"

"What is that?!" asked Elle. "This seems too confusing."

"Financial statement analysis is the process of determining if a company is a good buy versus a strong sell," explained Sam. "It helps investors like you more easily pick winners and losers."

"Really?!?" asked Elle.

"Yes! So let's get moving!" said Sam as he headed off deeper into the forest. "I need to show you my superpowers!"

"Owls don't have superpowers," said Elle, shaking her head.

"Well, every stock picker has five powers. I like to think of them as my superpowers, and if you listen carefully, I will pass them along to you," said Sam.

"Five powers!" said Elle.

"Yes, ugh, we have made it," said Sam.

"Okay, Sam. I'm ready," said Elle. "Share all of the powers. I've wanted to be a superhero my whole life!"

"This tree gives you the powers?!"
"No, it is something inside you," said Sam.
"Something you must always test and explore."

WELCOME

SAM

10

"Let's start with the basics," said Sam. "The stock I will give you is called AAPL. Do you know what AAPL does?"

"Huh? What is AAPL?" asked Elle, more confused than ever.

"AAPL is the ticker symbol for Apple," replied Sam.

"Apple the tech company, or the apple you eat?" asked Elle.

"Apple the tech company, of course," said Sam. "A ticker is a short symbol for a company. It's a way for people to look up a particular stock, which is critical when buying or selling stock."

"But where are my powers?" asked Elle.

POWER #1

"Well, power number one is right up your alley, Elle," said Sam. "It's Competitive Rivalry!"

"You're right," said Elle, laughing. "I am definitely competitive, but how is that a superpower?"

"Well, knowing your stock's competition is a major superpower," explained Sam.

"Why?" asked Elle.

"Because knowing who your company's competition is and how they compare to the business you own is critical!" said Sam. "It is the first step toward determining if your company has what it takes. For example, AAPL is a technology company and has many competitors. For the purpose of my example, we will explore two. The two competitors are...

Microsoft Corporation and Alphabet Inc.

"Microsoft Corporation (MSFT) is one of Apple's rivals! They also make computers and tablets. Alphabet Inc. (GOOGL) competes with Apple in many different markets. Google owns Android, so they compete in the smartphone market. Plus, Google Play competes with iTunes and they also both have online payment services that compete."

"I see. Stocks have competition, kind of like humans do in sports. But in sports, we have a score. What do stocks have to compare them against their competition?" asked Elle.

"Stocks have financial reports and ratios to compare themselves against one another, which is very similar to the score in a game. The numbers that companies report each quarter and each year serve as a way for investors to evaluate their success," said Sam. "Elle, do you know the saying, 'A team is only as good as its weakest player'?"

"Yeah!" said Elle, nodding her head and smiling.

"Well, a stock is only as good as its weakest report. You would want the MVP holding your money, right?" asked Sam.

"Yeah, only the best for me," said Elle.

"When evaluating a stock, we can't just look at the score at the end of the game, We have to look at tons of games, and tons of financial reports."

POWER #2

"Wow! That sounds fun!" said Elle. "So, what is power number two?"

"Supplier Power!" answered Sam.

"What is that?" asked Elle.

"Every business has a supplier, which is a company that helps provide the business with whatever is needed for their product," said Sam.

"This sounds kind of like when my school has a bake sale and my mom makes cookies," said Elle.

"Exactly! Your mom is your supplier. Now, can you guess who Apple's supplier is?"

17

"Hmm. Where can I start? They have so many different products," said Elle.

"Let's look at the screen on your watch," said Sam. "Who do you think makes that special screen?"

"It must be the supplier," said Elle.

"BINGO!" exclaimed Sam. "Analog Devices, Inc. (ADI) makes the screens for Apple watches & iPhones. But Apple has a huge number of suppliers that help them make all the products they sell."

18

"So are Apple's suppliers strong or weak?" asked Elle.

"The supplier's power to bargain with Apple is pretty low. Apple uses over 200 suppliers and if they had to switch one supplier for another, the cost to Apple would be relatively low. Since Apple is considered a major customer to most suppliers, Apple is the bigger fish in the pond."

"Over 200 suppliers!" exclaimed Elle. "That is one big fish! What's power number three?"

POWER #3

"Power number three is you. Look into the mirror," said Sam. "You purchase Apple products; you are a buyer. Power number three is Buyer Power!"

"My friend, so many people buy Apple products. Every kid on my soccer team has an iPad... How can I possibly measure each one against Apple?!" said Elle.

"There is your answer!" said Sam. "A single buyer would not have that much control over Apple's success. Individual bargaining power is weak and AAPL is once again strong."

"Okay, well, what if everyone decided that they no longer needed an iPad? Or an Apple Watch or iPhone? What if my whole soccer team and every kid in America was grounded, so the parents saw no need to buy an iPad?" asked Elle.

"Well, collectively, this would be a big deal, and the buyers' bargaining power would then be strong," said Sam.

"Well, luckily for Apple, their customers are loyal," said Elle.

"Exactly, that's another force that Apple must be mindful of, and they have proven to be," said Sam.

"How?" asked Elle.

"Just like in soccer, if you don't have a good defense, your team won't be entirely successful, right?" said Sam.

"Yeah, luckily, we have an amazing goalkeeper!" said Elle.

"Apple knows that if they don't keep their collective customers happy and updated, then they will be as good as gone in a couple of years. And then, they might not have enough time to grow their money," said Sam.

"So how is my stock on the defense?" asked Elle.

"Research and development! They are continually coming out with new versions and better products. This is Apple's defensive mechanism to retain buyers," said Sam.

"I see, so they have to make sure they are one step ahead of the competition," said Elle.

"Exactly! Which brings us to superpower number four!" exclaimed Sam.

"The threat of someone replacing them?" guessed Elle.

"Yes! The threat of substitution!"

POWER
#4

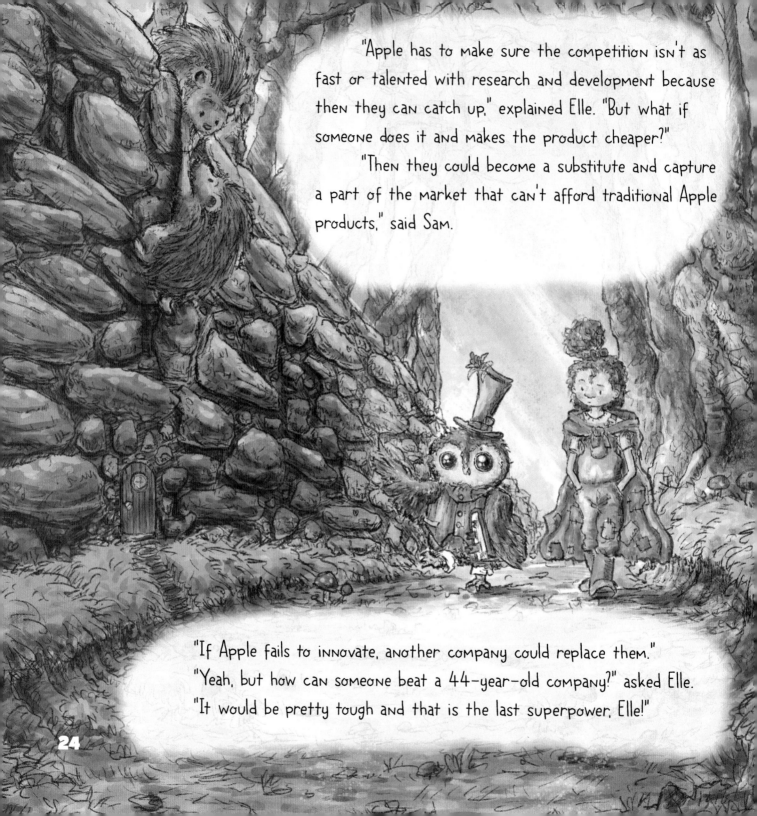

"Apple has to make sure the competition isn't as fast or talented with research and development because then they can catch up," explained Elle. "But what if someone does it and makes the product cheaper?"

"Then they could become a substitute and capture a part of the market that can't afford traditional Apple products," said Sam.

"If Apple fails to innovate, another company could replace them."
"Yeah, but how can someone beat a 44-year-old company?" asked Elle.
"It would be pretty tough and that is the last superpower, Elle!"

24

"Knowing the threat of new competition?" asked Elle.

"Yep!" said Sam. "The threat of new companies entering the same market!"

"Wow, so kinda like when a new girl joined our soccer team. I didn't want her to be better than me," said Elle.

"Haha! Yes, Elle!" said Sam. "Apple does not make it easy for new companies to enter the market to compete with them. They are constantly entering new markets and expanding their product offering. They are constantly practicing and evolving."

25

"So Apple's superpower score is 5 out of 5!" exclaimed Elle.

"That's right. These powers are also known as Porter's Five Forces," said Sam, "which is typically step one in financial statement analysis, and the most crucial step to understanding your stock."

"Does the superpower test work for any stock?" asked Elle.

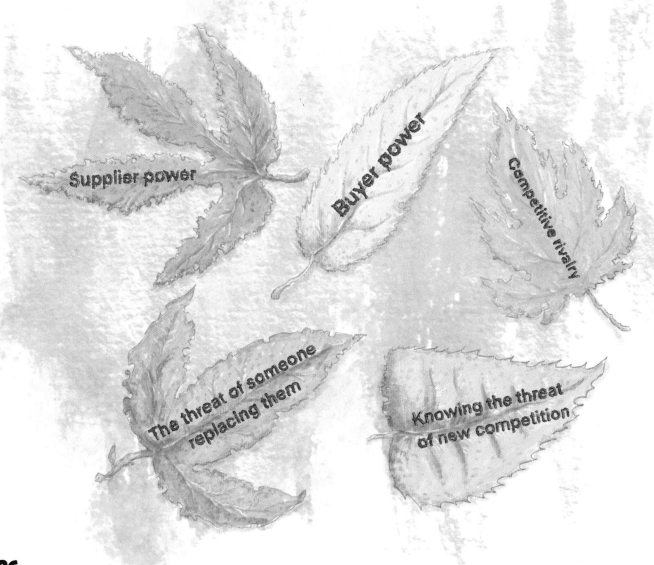

"Yes, so now that you have the fundamentals of Porter's Five Forces, you can begin exploring all companies that interest you!" said Sam. "Congratulations!"

"So, I can't eat a stock, see a stock, or wear a stock. But I can explore what I eat, explore products I see, and explore products I wear because odds are those companies are stocks or in some way related to stocks!" said Elle.

"Precisely," said Sam.

"Thanks, friend!" said Elle. "I can't wait to explore my next stock!"

THE END!

PORTER'S FIVE FORCES

- Competitive Rivalry - How strong is your competition?
- Supplier Power - Who are your company's suppliers and how powerful are they at dictating price?
- Buyer Power - The pressure consumers can exert on businesses to get them to provide higher quality products, better customer service, and lower prices.
- The Threat of Substitution - The threat of another product being able to replace your stock's product.
- The Threat of New Entrants - How easy is it for a brand-new company to enter the market?

DISCLOSURE

ABOUT THE AUTHOR

Nicolette DiMaggio is the author & founder of Stock Explore. She writes stories to inspire the next generation of investors. Nicolette received her BS in Finance from Siena College and is currently an equity research associate for Willis Towers Watson. Her day job consists of meeting with some of the most brilliant investment minds today, covering U.S. equities.

Stock Explore's mission is to inspire the next generation of investors. Learn more about Nicolette and Stock Explore at www.Stock-Explore.com

ABOUT THE ILLUSTRATOR

Ethan Roffler: As a kid who grew up in the rainy Seattle area, I spent a lot of time stuck inside plotting world domination and the downfall of my siblings, so I learned at an early age to embrace my creative side. As I grew older, my love for art grew right along with me! I remember the excitement when our local newspaper published several of the comic strips I created, and I knew that being an artist was the most amazing thing in the world!

Being a freelance artist means I get to participate in all sorts of creative projects (from weird and wonderful concepts to strange and mysterious characters). It's seriously the best being able to do what I love for a living! Although I love each project dearly, I hold the opportunity to illustrate children's books very close to my heart, even more now that I have two little people/minions of my own.

GLOSSARY

Stock - A piece of ownership in a company.

Stock certificate - A legal document that certifies ownership of a specific number of shares in a corporation. Paper certificates aren't as prevalent today but are symbolic of a stock.

Investment time horizon - The total length of time a security is anticipated to be held by an investor. For example: The investment time horizon for a child is much longer than an adult because they are anticipated to live longer.

Proxy - A letter sent out to investors to vote or comment on the way their stock's being run.

Technological obsolescence - When a new product has been created to replace an older version.

10K Report - A corporation's annual report, summarizing financial performance for the year. This is a useful tool for investors to follow as it contains important information on the company's financial health.

Research & development - Innovative activities that are undertaken by corporations in developing new services or products, or improving existing services or products.

Innovation - The action of developing a new method, idea or product.

Financial analysis - The process of evaluating businesses to determine their suitability.

Financial reports - Formal records of financial activities.

Management - The administration of an organization. (i.e. CEO, CFO, COO)

Board of directors - A group of individuals who supervise an organization.

Supply chain - This is a system of organizations, people, activities, information, and resources involved in moving a product or service from supplier to customer.